7 Principles to Developing and Maintaining Your Passion

7 Principles to Developing and Maintaining Your Passion

Connect to Your Purpose | Cultivate Your Vision | Create Your Plan

GENEVIEVE KUMAPLEY
MARGARET ALABI

Genevieve
I dedicate this book to my wonderful husband, Robert, who is extremely supportive and my greatest advocate. Sena, Delali and Nicholas, my three children, you bring out the best in me, for that I thank God for your lives. To my parents, Bernard and Mary, thank you for raising me to always seek to give and do my best. To all MyGOAL Autism and Agape House of Worship family, thank you so for your love and support.

Margaret
This book is dedicated to my father and mother Patrick and Selia Alabi. Their patience, love and continuous encouragement help me to be a better person everyday. To my younger brother David, your cool and calm demeanor helps to keep me grounded. Last but not least, my baby sister Rachael, you challenge me to be my best. I love each one of you dearly!

Connect to Your Purpose, Cultivate Your Vision and Create Your Plan

ACKNOWLEDGEMENTS

Thank you to
Pastor Loraine Priestley-Smith, Megan Brown, Tunji Olatubosun and
Sola Osofisan who proofed and edited our manuscript.

INTRODUCTION

P.A.S.S.I.O.N.
You're probably thinking to yourself if I could be doing xyz right now... my life would be so much better. Our question for you is why aren't you doing it?

This devotional is intended to activate the passion and dream resting in you so that you can begin to fulfill God's purpose for your life. It will give you the practical tools necessary to connect, cultivate and establish your dream. These 7 principles can be studied over several days, weeks or months. The goal is to interact with each principle. Simply put, developing and maintaining your passion should not be a onetime process! In each section, there are personal stories aimed to highlight how we as authors have gone through and in some cases are still going through the process. At the end of each principle you will find prayers (plug-in's) to activate what God is telling you, along with suggested action points to take your passion to the next level. We hope this devotional will serve as a tool for you to discover what God has created you to do.

How do you know when you are living a life of purpose?
"We have different gifts, according to the grace given us. If a man's gift is prophesying, let him use it in proportion to his faith. [7] If it is serving, let him serve; if it is teaching, let him teach; [8] if it is encouraging, let him encourage; if it is contributing to the needs of others, let him give generously; if it is to lead, do it diligently; if it is to show mercy, do it cheerfully."
Romans 12:6-8 (NIV)

"For we are God's masterpiece. He has created us anew in Christ Jesus, so we can do the good things he planned for us long ago."
Ephesians 2:10 (NLT)

Our Story

Genevieve's:

In 2006, when I thought of starting a project related to my son's diagnosis, I didn't quite know how I was going to make it happen. As I waited patiently in the doctor's lounge for my son to finish his therapy appointment, I began to put my thoughts on paper. I began to conceive the vision and mission of an organization that would eventually be birthed in 2008. My next step was to ask a friend to create a logo, which he did; but I filed it for later use. Interestingly, I didn't take the project seriously at that time.

Two years later, I began to feel this burning desire to learn more about myself and get closer to God. This "push" led me to speak with individuals from a spiritual perspective, which eventually led to my enrollment into a Bible school. "History Maker's Bible School" was very untraditional; it challenged us as students to draw on our desires and passions to make a difference in the world. Confronted with the opportunity and challenge, I decided to revisit the idea I had in 2006 and developed a plan that I began to implement prior to graduation from the History Maker's Bible School. I shared the idea with key supporters who directed, encouraged, and coached me to start a 501(c)(3) non-profit organization dedicated to supporting families affected by autism.

Margaret's:

The year was 2009, I was in my 3rd year of pharmacy school and I was becoming more involved in the city of New Orleans and its happenings. I was being exposed to a number of entrepreneurs and their stories and I was inspired to do something! I started to build a business plan and reached out to people in my community to help grow my idea. Long story short, I partnered with a friend for all of the wrong reasons and found out in the process that we did not share the same value system. God, being sovereign, delivered me out of that situation unscathed.

I thought that my hopes of being an entrepreneur were dashed. I moved to New Jersey in 2011 to complete a post-doctoral fellowship and felt like I would never have the time or energy to devote to my own business. While completing my fellowship, God began to touch my heart in the area of business again and honestly I was a little apprehensive. I did not seriously start to re-engage in the building of my branding/marketing business again until 2012. This time, instead of going into this process with my human knowledge, I relied heavily on God and asked Him to guide me. After all, He was the one who blessed me with the idea anyway! To get started, God instructed me to offer my services free of charge to a non-profit that He later identified as MyGOAL Autism.

Today, I am growing in knowledge, wisdom and understanding in areas where I don't have any formal training. I'm doing things that I never knew I could because of my supporters who provide my business with new challenges daily.

Connect to Your Purpose
"For I know the plans I have for You, Says the Lord"
Jeremiah 29:11 (NLT)

Principle #1 ◉
PERCEPTION: HEIGHTEN YOUR LEVEL OF AWARENESS

This is the burning desire in a person to make a difference in the lives of others. It is getting to understand your call and the reason for which you exist.

"Jesus gave them this answer: "Very truly I tell you, the Son can do nothing by himself; he can do only what he sees his Father doing, because whatever the Father does the Son also does." John 5:19 (NIV)

"Now therefore, O sons, listen to me, For blessed are they who keep my ways. Heed instruction and be wise, And do not neglect it. Blessed is the man who listens to me, Watching daily at my gates, Waiting at my doorposts." Proverbs 8:32-34 (NASB)

Our Story:
Genevieve's:
In 2006, my creative abilities were actualized through the History Makers Bible School. I was challenged to channel my pain into a positive platform that would motivate people who have similar struggles as me; I even gave it a name! Of course, at that time I didn't know how that was going to materialize until 2 years later.

Margaret's:
There were so many good things happening in New Orleans right after Hurricane Katrina in 2006 and I wanted to be involved. My entrepreneurial spirit began to bubble up and I became acutely aware of my ability to promote people and events. I did it successfully on campus and it brought me joy so I decided to partner with a girlfriend of mine to bring a marketing company to life for New Orleans small business sector.

Heighten Your Level of Awareness
God has created each of us to fulfill a particular purpose! If you have yet to reach this conclusion, I suggest you read Rick Warren's *The Purpose Driven Life*. Understanding your purpose in life is a great start to identifying your passion. Your purpose is why you exist and your passion is how your purpose is manifested on earth. It engages every faculty of your mind to heighten your level of awareness

(perception) and attracts you to a cause, issue or business that arouses a flurry of emotions within you.

For example, what are the things that incite anger, joy, and excitement within you? Are you angered by injustice? Are you moved to tears when someone is in emotional or physical pain? What makes you feel valued? Your passion could be tied to these emotions. This attraction process is often an important indicator of God's divine plan for you and all of His children.

What do you hear God telling you to do?

That is a loaded question, typically followed by more questions, so ask yourself:

1. What do you think God has created you to do?
2. What is the one thing that people always say you do well?
3. What are you most fearful of when it comes to your passion?
4. What are you willing to invest in yourself to bring this passion to bear?

It's important to ask yourself these questions. I'm sure Gideon wished he had. Read the story of Gideon: Judges 6-7. Sometimes we don't see ourselves the way God sees us or even the way others see us. While the Angel of God told Gideon he was a mighty man of valor, he didn't see himself that way. Remember, if God gives you a desire, He also gives you the ability to carry it out!

Plug-in:

- Lord whatever you are doing, don't do it without me.
- Open my eyes to perceive what you would like me to do and when you would like me to do it.
- Lord grant me the spirit of discernment to connect to what you are saying to me.
- Lord bring to my remembrance every idea, dream and project that you have given me.
- Lord birth through me now a company, tools, solutions, inventions, and scientific discoveries that solve problems and meet human needs.

Now What?

- Brainstorm and jot down any and every idea that comes to mind. What problem do you wish you could have a solution to?
- If you could solve it, how would you go about it?
- What is the one thing you would like to be and do if money or other responsibilities were not an obstacle or an issue?
- What are your gifts?
- What do you enjoy that brings joy or relief to others?

Reflection Notes:

_____

_____

_____

_____

_____

_____

_____

_____

_____

_____

_____

_____

_____

_____

_____

_____

Principle #2

ASSESSMENT: WHAT IS IT GOING TO GET STARTED?

This is the research stage. It is about identifying what tools are needed to accomplish what God is calling you to do.

"My people perish for lack of knowledge." Hosea 4:6 (KJV)

"I thought, "These are only the poor; they are foolish, for they do not know the way of the LORD, the requirements of their God." Jeremiah 5:4 (NIV)

"Suppose one of you wants to build a tower. What is the first thing you will do? Won't you sit down and figure out how much it will cost and if you have enough money to pay for it?" Luke 14:28 (CEV)

"Zeal must be accompanied by knowledge." Romans 10:2 (NIV) Paraphrased

Our Story:

Genevieve's:

Once I enrolled in the History Maker's Bible school, I was challenged to start on my dream. What was helpful was hearing the testimony of other people who had started to work on their dreams. Part of the project to complete the certification program was creating and establishing a plan of how I would actualize my dream. This required some research on my part and eventually I was able to outline the vision of what I wanted to see happen.

Margaret's:

My partner and I were at odds about this particular step and this is where my initial business idea failed. Being unequally yoked is not unique to marriage only; it applies to all relationships and partnerships, which I learned the hard way. After I completed pharmacy school I moved to a new state, with new needs, and was surprised to find that my business idea was still viable. I began to speak with small business owners to determine how I could help. It took me a year to really nail down my business model and I'm glad I took the time!

What is it Going to Take to Get Started?
You now know and understand why you exist and it's definitely to "Do Something"! Now it's time to face the good, the bad and the ugly associated with making your passion palpable. Take the time to consider the joys and challenges of embarking on this journey. The use of a framework such as what is outlined below can help lay a firm foundation. Detailed planning helps eliminate fear of the unknown.

HOW - *Do you need a business plan? What is it going to cost you?*
WHAT - *Is your passion a non-profit or for profit entity? Is it a job, ministry or project?*
WHO - *Who are you serving? Who is currently working in this space? Are there associations/societies you can join to gain more knowledge?*
WHEN - *Can you get started right now? When do you expect to launch your vision?*
WHERE - *Is this a local, national or global effort? Do you need a physical office or working space?*

While these steps are critical, it is easy to get stuck in the assessment phase. Don't over-assess! Take a note from the parable that Jesus shared in Matthew 19:16-22 about the rich young ruler. He hesitated too long to assess what selling everything would mean and he missed out on the opportunity of a lifetime.

Plug-in:
- Lord, I know what I am called to do but I don't know where and how to begin. Direct and teach me the way I should go. Please order my steps and attitude to learning.
- Lord grant me the grace to sit and assess and count the costs involved in what I am about embark on.
- Lord baptize and fill me with the spirit of wisdom to know how to execute and actualize the dream you have given me.

Now What?

- Enroll in a course, attend seminars, read books and understand the role.
- Research groups or individuals who have done the same thing.

Reflection Notes:

_____

_____

_____

_____

_____

_____

_____

_____

_____

_____

_____

_____

_____

_____

Cultivate Your Vision
"Where there is no vision, the people perish"
Proverbs 29:18 (KJV)

Principle #3

SHARE: EXPOSE OTHERS TO YOUR VISION

One's vision can only be revealed through vulnerability, open and candid conversation. Don't share with just anyone unless you are confident that the time is right.

"Plans are established by seeking advice; so if you wage war, obtain guidance."
Proverbs 20:18 (NIV)

"The way of a fool is right in his own eyes, But a wise man is he who listens to counsel."
Proverbs 12:15 (NIV)

"Do not give that which is holy (the sacred thing) to the dogs, and do not throw your pearls before hogs, lest they trample upon them with their feet and turn and tear you in pieces."
Matthew 7:6 (NIV)

Our Story:

Genevieve's:

After registering the organization, I prayed about who to bring on board and began sharing the vision with a number of people. I reached out to my pastors, mentors and friends. We formed a board of directors and advisors. A few months later, we formally launched the organization and invited people to join us on the journey. My dream became a reality because I shared it with the right people at the right time.

Margaret's:

This time around, I was very particular about whom I shared my vision with and how I shared it. With prayer and supplication, I asked God to provide me with a group of people who I can discuss my dreams and vision with and in 2013, He blessed me with a prayer group of women and one of the women happened to be my first client.

Expose Others to Your Vision

Once you have bought into your own vision, you should begin to share it with others. This is best done in an informal setting with people that you trust to give you constructive feedback. It allows you to speak to the **why** of your vision without feeling pressured to communicate the **what** and **how**. Show your confidence by speaking to what truly excites you about your vision. Two keys to this stage of the process are timing and managing your state of mind. These allow you to receive and implement the comments given.

Consider the story of Paul in the Book of Acts and how he single-handedly established the early church in the New Testament. He shared his vision with Barnabas, John, Mark, Luke, Priscilla and Aquila, to name a few, they were pivotal to his success

Never discount your ability to influence others by sharing. Your story will empower others and make them feel connected to you.

Plug-in:
- Lord, please give me the boldness to step out to share my vision and dreams.
- Surround me with Godly men and women who can offer the counsel and direction I need.
- Holy Spirit, grant me the joy and confidence to take the right steps to actualize my dream.

Now What?
- Share your story and vision with those in your circle of influence.
- Record the feedback and incorporate it into the vision where necessary.

Reflection Notes:

Principle #4

SUPPORTERS: WHO'S GOT YOUR BACK?
Sharing the vision can lead to gaining some key supporters.

"Plans fail for lack of counsel, but with many advisers they succeed."
Proverbs 15:22 (NIV)

"For lack of guidance a nation falls, but victory is won through many advisers." Proverbs 11:14 (NIV)

Our Story:
Genevieve's:
I found out the hard way that supporters fall into 3 categories: The ACEs, The Core and The Seasonal (I expound more on these in the 'Who's Got Your Back Section") I met individuals who pretended to care but quickly showed themselves as only interested in drawing from the organization. On the other hand, I gained some wonderful people who became very close to me and now are part of the Core supporters. The ACE supporters have been instrumental in getting access to resources. The key thing I have learned is staying connected with them and treating them based on where they are. I remember one incident where one of the seasonal supporters started to treat me unkindly as result of me not promoting her agenda specifically. She started out as a member of the board but over a period of months, I noticed that she was not forward thinking in her association with the organization. Her presence on the board had become a bad fit, but I left it in God's hands, and He made a way. Soon enough, she confessed to being frustrated and resigned. God always shows us who is with us and who is not. We just need to be patient and alert.

Margaret's:
Supporters make a world of difference, especially when you feel like you can't make it another day. Over the past year, my Core supporters have carried me through my highs and lows. They tell me the truth even when I don't want to hear it. This matters because, my many conversations with the Core prepares me for rewarding encounters with my ACEs.

Who's Got Your Back?

You've captured the attention of many by sharing your vision and now they would like to know how they can support you. This is a great stage to be in because we all need supporters!

Be sure to identify where your supporters stand based on the categories below:

a. *ACE Supporters-* These are the "Pauls", Individuals at the highest height of their career and they take joy in developing others and believe in what you are doing. You call on them during the critical periods for expert advice. Use this card sparingly.

b. *Core supporters* – These are key individuals who are like Barnabas in your life. They are your encouragers. They know the day-to-day stuff that goes on. They cheer you on and pray with you when things are not going right.

c. *Seasonal Supporters* – These are people who are around for a season or for their own personal gain. Understand that they may be looking for something in return for helping you. You should support their vision and expect them to support yours.

Plug-in:

- Lord, open my eyes to know those who are called to be my Core Supporters, those who are seasonal supporters and those who are the ACES.
- Lord, please create an opportunity for me to interact with people who fit into all these categories in Jesus name.
- Help me cultivate and nurture the relationships that are instrumental in developing and advancing the work of your kingdom in Jesus name.

Now What?

- Categorize your contacts and engage with them based on where they fall on your hierarchy of supporters
- Engage with supporters by sharing your progress in a consistent fashion (for example, a monthly or quarterly update)

Reflection Notes:

_____

_____

_____

_____

_____

_____

_____

_____

_____

_____

_____

_____

_____

Principle #5 💡

INSIGHTS: EXPLORE AND VALIDATE

Know and understand what interests your target audience. You can gain key insights from those you are serving. What and how are they feeling? Conducting surveys and getting feedback is critical to being relevant.

"From the tribe of Issachar, there were 200 leaders of the tribe with their relatives. All these men understood the signs of the times and knew the best course for Israel to take." 1 Chronicles 12:32 (NLV)

"This you know, my beloved brethren. But everyone must be quick to hear, slow to speak and slow to anger" James 1:19 (NASB)

"Then, after three days they found Him in the temple, sitting in the midst of the teachers, both listening to them and asking them questions." Luke 2:46 (NASB)

"Since it was customary for the king to consult experts in matters of law and justice, he spoke with the wise men who understood the times." Esther 1:13 (NIV)

Our Story

Genevieve's:

The best insights gained have been bringing people with the expertise to the team to ask the hard questions. Our board consistently challenges me as a leader to consider various options and ways to improve. At each meeting, I bring the report of what we have been doing and what new endeavors we are pursuing. This process has grown my organization and aided my personal growth as a leader.

Margaret's:

I use my clients to provide me with feedback based on the personalized services my company provides to them. I also use my core supporters to provide me with valuable feedback. I am still working on a formalized feedback loop and currently use a standard set of questions to gather the information necessary to help me grow.

Explore and Validate

Depending on your outlook, this can undoubtedly be one of the most exciting or disheartening parts of the process. The word insight has

16

many definitions. For the purposes of this book we will ascribe to the following: *Knowledge in the form of perspective, understanding, or deduction[1].* Are you ready to begin your exploration of the good, the bad and the ugly? Let's start by identifying how much you already know and what you want to know more about. The best way to do this is to take a moment to reflect on your:

1. Purpose (why are you doing this?)
2. Passion (what is it that you're doing?)
3. Plan (who/how you're serving?)

Now, let's go back to Principle 2 - Assessment. Develop the information you gathered from this section into strategic questions that will help you validate your insights for an ideal outcome. Consider the story of David in 1 Samuel 30:8. After returning home to Ziklag to find his town pillaged, he asked simple direct questions of God, the one he served. "Should I pursue these raiders? Will I overtake them?" To which the Lord replied to him, "Pursue them, for you will certainly overtake them and rescue the people."

Keep in mind that the answer may not always be a resounding yes, but the insights gathered will:
-Help you to see things from the perspective of your audience of interest.
-Act as a checkpoint for you to determine your effectiveness.
-Identify if what you're doing is working, if not, try another approach.
-Determine what needs to happen moving forward.

Plug-in:
- Lord, help me to be relevant to the needs of those I am called to serve. Grant me the desire to seek insights and help me to continuously review and reassess my effectiveness.

---

1. (http://www.businessdictionary.com/definition/insight.html)

Now What?
- Develop a system to collect information on the process, progress and success of your efforts (i.e. engage your team, customers and those you serve in a dialogue)
- Commit to a quarterly plan and be intentional about reviewing and celebrating your progress.
- Build on your current knowledge and sharpen the tools of your trade

Reflection Notes:

_____

_____

_____

_____

_____

_____

_____

_____

_____

_____

_____

_____

_____

_____

_____

_____

_____

Create Your Plan
"Commit to the Lord whatever you do, and your plans will succeed"
 Proverbs 16:3 (NIV)

Principle #6

ORGANIZE: EXECUTION IS FLAWLESS WITH A LITTLE BIT OF ORGANIZATION

Be detailed and organized. Setting up strong organizational structures is necessary for success. Plan your work and work your plan, this ensures growth and greater expansion.

"And the LORD answered me, and said, Write the vision, and make [it] plain upon tables, that he may run that readeth it". Habakkuk 2:2 (KJV)

"For God is not [the author] of confusion, but of peace, as in all churches of the saints." 1 Corinthians 14:33 (KJV)

Our Story:

Genevieve's:

This is an area of my greatest strength, however, I noticed after two years of getting things done, I started to slack off and sometimes postponed doing what works. The end results were mistakes, and loss of time and resources. It pays to be organized. If you are lacking in this area, pray that God will bring you people that can teach you or support you.

Margaret's:

Organization is my best friend and my worst enemy! Planning and organizing is not a one-time thing. The key to success is to continuously check and update the plan to reflect the challenges and wins. This is an area where I'm still growing and am grateful for the project planning tools out there!

Execution is Flawless with a Little Bit of Organization

Organization is key! You must cultivate habits that enable you to be a self-starter. Decide from this moment forth that you have no business with procrastination. Take advantage of project management tools that are freely available online to help you determine what success looks like. Become best friends with your calendar; create a reasonable timeline that will help you achieve your goals, one step at a time. With this is hand you can be productive and execute your plan flawlessly! In the Bible, one of the best examples of organization is Paul's establishment of the church in the New Testament. Paul was not able to physically set these churches up, so he enlisted the help of two young men by the name of Timothy and Titus. In 3 detailed letters to these men, Paul laid out the positions that he knew would be paramount in maintaining order and promoting the true word of God. Timothy and Titus were able to successfully establish churches in Ephesus, Spain, Rome and Crete because Paul provided them with a clear and organized plan

Plug-in:
- Lord, please shine your light on my life and highlight my strengths and weakness.
- Help me to explore ways to grow through steps that I put in place. Send me helpers who are strong in the areas where I am weak.
- Expose areas in my life or mission where there is disorder or inefficiencies.
- Thank you for reminding me each moment of everyday is critical to my success.

Now What?
- Invest in resources to help you be organized such as project planning tools, apps or software.
- Identify tools of the trade that help you to be more productive.
- Keep track of appointments and identify future opportunities
- Know and understand your strengths and invest in boosting areas of weakness.

Reflection Notes:

_____

_____

_____

_____

_____

_____

_____

_____

_____

_____

_____

_____

_____

_____

NETWORK: WHO YOU KNOW WILL HELP YOU GROW

Every interaction with any person is an open door to greater expansion. The ultimate goal in expansion and capacity building is all about optimizing the networks to which you are connected. Attend trade shows and programs in your field of expertise and expand the range of people you can meet.

"Not neglecting to meet together, as is the habit of some, but encouraging one another, and all the more as you see the Day drawing near."
Hebrews 10:25 (ESV)

"Two are better than one, because they have a good reward for their toil. For if they fall, one will lift up his fellow. But woe to him who is alone when he falls and has not another to lift him up! Again, if two lie together, they keep warm, but how can one keep warm alone? And though a man might prevail against one who is alone, two will withstand him—a threefold cord is not quickly broken."
Ecclesiastes 4:9-12 (ESV)

"And let us consider how to stir up one another to love and good works."
Hebrews 10:24 (ESV)

Our Story:
Genevieve's:
The amazing part of this dream and journey is coming out of my shell and learning to connect with people. I have met all kinds of people simply by my willingness to venture out of my comfort zone and share with people. I have met men and women from all spheres of life who have directed me to other people because I opened my mouth to say hello and share my story.

Margaret's:
Networking is one of my favorite things to do! I truly enjoy meeting new people and learning about who they are and what they do! I take this approach because networking is not just about what's in it for me; I use it as an opportunity to offer myself as a resource. I've learned that when you present yourself as a resource, it opens doors to many opportunities and allows your network to promote you. My network is strong because I built it that way! I don't make it a point to know everybody, because I would never get any work done, but I do make it a

point to know the right people. Knowing the right people ensures that everybody else knows you!

Who You Know Will Help You Grow
When you think of the word network, think of it as fellowshipping, which leads to relationship building. This is not a check the box task. This is truly about connecting with and getting to know a person. Remember people like to work with people they know. Look for the smiling person in the room and engage them in conversation. Take it one person at a time. Jesus was a master at this. Little did Zacchaeus know that when he climbed into that tree, he became the proverbial smiling person in the room who Jesus gravitated towards. Jesus (in his humanity) had no clue about who Zacchaeus was but the crowd around him wasted no time in sharing that Zacchaeus was a well-known sinner. Jesus, being no respecter of persons insisted that he wanted to be acquainted with Zacchaeus nonetheless. By so doing, Jesus had instant influence with Zacchaeus who was the head tax collector. This in turn would extend to all of the tax collectors that he managed. See how Jesus worked that? You too can do the same!

Plug-in:
* Dear Lord, thank you for setting up encounters for me in advance. I pray that I will be mentally present in all interactions and encounters you set up for me. I will see each person I meet as part of your plan to establish the purpose you have for me on this earth.

Now What?
- List creative ways and places to connect with people to expand your circle of influence.
- Solicit your group of supporters to connect and promote you within their network.

Reflection Notes:

_____

_____

_____

_____

_____

_____

_____

_____

_____

_____

_____

_____

_____

_____

_____

_____

CONCLUSION

Your life is best assessed by the impact you make and is a function of how much zeal and passion you put into what you do. Passion is both an attitude and a lifestyle. Once you find your footing where God has placed you, the rest is to *hear, tell* and *share your vision.* The zeal for doing God's best in this world must consume us.

"Therefore, brothers, be all the more diligent to make your calling and election sure, for if you practice these qualities you will never fall."
2 Peter 1:10 (ESV)

"Everyone who comes to Me and hears My words and acts on them, I will show you whom he is like: he is like a man building a house, who dug deep and laid a foundation on the rock; and when a flood occurred, the torrent burst against that house and could not shake it, because it had been well built. But the one who has heard and has not acted accordingly, is like a man who built a house on the ground without any foundation; and the torrent burst against it and immediately it collapsed, and the ruin of that house was great."
Luke 6:47-49 (NASB)

ABOUT THE AUTHORS

Genevieve Kumapley is a Founder & Executive Director of MyGOAL, a non-profit Autism organization in the United States that supports families facing Autism by providing resources and connections. MyGOAL conducts programs locally, and through it's global initiative, the Haven International Project in Ghana, West Africa. Both the domestic and international programs provide training and education for care providers (professionals, teachers and parents) of individuals with Autism and other Intellectual Disabilities.

She received her Doctor of Pharmacy Degree with Honors from the University of Illinois at Chicago in 1998. Genevieve is a Board Certified Oncology Pharmacist and practices at a hospital, in New Brunswick. She also holds an Adjunct Clinical Professor appointment with Rutgers University Ernest Mario School of Pharmacy and trains Doctor of Pharmacy students.

Genevieve serves as a Professional Advisory Board member of the Sisters' Network of Central New Jersey, a Breast Cancer Survivor Group. She is also the Vice President of the Board of Directors of Touch Link, a Domestic Violence, non-profit organization. She is committed to helping individuals discover and start-up their dreams. Genevieve has received awards for her leadership and service from several organizations including the 2013 Role Model Award from the Roselle Branch of the NAACP.

She is married to Robert and they have 3 children (Sena, Nicholas who was diagnosed with Autism in 2003 and Delali). Genevieve is a passionate worshipper of Jesus Christ and serves at RCCG Agape House of Worship as a Minister in the Healing, Special Needs, Prayer and Marriage Ministries. She is a co-author of the book anthology, "*Network to Increase your Net Worth*" and her chapter is titled, No Passion, No Gain. She has been featured on several TV and Radio Networks including ABC , GTV and NJN.

Margaret A. Alabi is the founder and CEO of Meje7 LLC, a consulting firm that was birthed out of her passion for helping people identify and achieve their purpose. With extensive pharmaceutical industry experience, she has held various roles that involve listening to the needs of patients, and enabling healthcare providers, communities and organizations to work together in new ways to address critical issues and significantly impact patient health, specifically in the area of diabetes.

In the spring of 2011 Margaret completed her Doctorate of Pharmacy at Xavier University of Louisiana, College of Pharmacy where she held leadership positions on a local and national level. Upon graduating she received the University Service Key Award for her commitment to service on and off the campus. Margaret is an Albert Schweitzer Fellow for Life and an alumna of the Rutgers Pharmaceutical Industry Fellowship Program, where she served as the Community Development Chair and was responsible for fostering the professional and social development of over 70 fellows and 300 plus alumni.

In her spare time, Margaret volunteers as member of the MyGOAL Autism Advisory Board and serves as a public speaker, leadership coach and personal brand specialist to local organizations, small businesses, educational institutions and high potential individuals.

Originally from Atlanta, Georgia, Margaret is still settling into New Jersey and this is made easier through her spiritual home Agape House of Worship where she currently serves as the Youth ministry leader and member of the Singles, Healing and Prayer ministries.

Resources

We have listed some resources here to help you develop and maintain your passion:

The best source of inspiration that we have found is the Holy Bible.
www.biblegateway.com

Identify your strengths using Gallup's StrengthsFinders 2.0.
www.gallupstrengthscenter.com

Looking to start a business or non-profit based on your passion? Check out the Small Business Administration.
www.sba.gov

Get your business ready for launch with resources from Start Up Nation.
www.startupnation.com

Find additional inspiration from the books below

From Passion to Execution: How to Start and Grow an Effective Nonprofit Organization by Lyn Scott

Fundraising Basics: A Complete Guide by Barbara Ciconte